Daily Life in the INDUS VALLEY CIVILIZATION

Brian Williams

raintree

a Capstone company — publishers for children

Raintree is an imprint of Capstone Global Library Limited, a company incorporated in England and Wales having its registered office at 7 Pilgrim Street, London, EC4V 6LB – Registered company number: 6695582

www.raintree.co.uk
myorders@raintree.co.uk

Edited by Linda Staniford and Holly Beaumont
Designed by Philippa Jenkins
Original illustrations © Capstone Global Library Limited 2015
Illustrated by HL Studios, Witney, Oxon; caption character and pages 42-43 by Philippa Jenkins
Picture research by Gina Kammer
Production by Victoria Fitzgerald
Originated by Capstone Global Library Ltd
Printed and bound in China by Leo Paper Products

ISBN 978 1 406 29851 2
19 18 17 16 15
10 9 8 7 6 5 4 3 2 1

British Library Cataloguing in Publication Data
A full catalogue record for this book is available from the British Library.

Acknowledgements
We would like to thank the following for permission to reproduce photographs: Alamy: © Angelo Hornak, 17, © Mike Goldwater, 9, © Robert Harding Picture Library Ltd, 10, (top) 37, © World Religions Photo Library, 14; Art Resource, N.Y.: © RMN-Grand Palais, 27; Corbis: © Angelo Hornak, 31, © Angelo Hornak, 36, © Diego Lezama Orezzoli, 5, © Paul Almasy, 23, 42, The Art Archive/© Alfredo Dagli Orti, 38; Getty Images: DEA/C.BEVILACQUA, 32, DEA/G. NIMATALLAH, 7, 34, Dorling Kindersley, 20, 35, Leemage, 29; Glow Images: Heritage Images/CM Dixon, 6, Heritage Images/CM Dixon, 30; Newscom: Frank Bienewald imageBROKER, 24, Joseph Martin, (bottom) 37, REUTERS/AMIT DAVE, 22, Robert Harding Productions, 18, 19, Robert Harding/Robert Francis, 40, Universal Images Group Universal Images Group/Leemage, 39, cover, World History Archive, 28; Shutterstock: JoeyPhoto, 41, Phaendin, 33.

Cover image: A clay model of a bullock cart from the ancient Indus city of Mohenjo-Daro. It is now kept at the Karachi Museum, Pakistan.

We would like to thank Dr Mark Manuel for his help in the preparation of this book.

CONTENTS

Some words are shown in bold, **like this**. You can find out what they mean by looking in the glossary.

About 5,000 years ago (in around 2500 BC), people built cities beside the Indus River in the Indian subcontinent. The Indus, once known as "the king river" in ancient Indian literature, rises in the Himalayan mountains, and flows 2,900 kilometres (1,800 miles) to the Arabian Sea. The longest river of modern Pakistan, its waters are important for **irrigation**. The Indus provides water for crops and animals, and routes for trade. The Indus Valley was a good place to build a **civilization**.

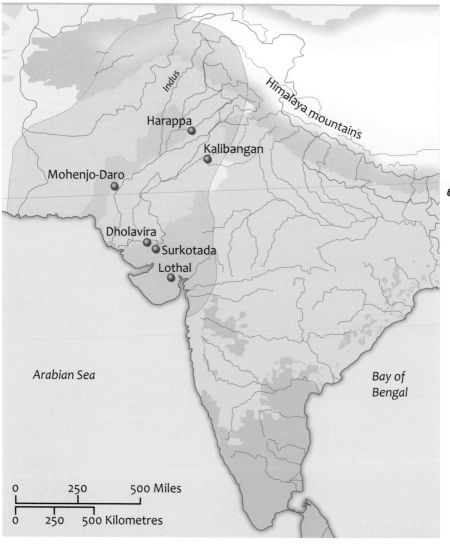

This map shows the Indus Valley culture region. People settled beside the rivers that flow from the Himalayan Mountains south into the Arabian Sea.

Rivers and cities

The first civilizations grew near great rivers: in Sumer, Egypt, China and in the Indus Valley. People built cities and developed writing, arts and crafts, trade links, religions and governments. Indus cities, such as Mohenjo-Daro and Harappa, were among the finest in Asia. There were many Indus cities, near other rivers as far north as Afghanistan and southeast into India. We don't know much about the people who built these cities, and whose ancient way of life shaped the culture of modern India and Pakistan.

Little remains of Indus cities, but we can see where streets and houses once stood. At Harappa, railway-builders in the 1800s took away so many bricks that little was left for archaeologists to study.

SLOW PROGRESS

Indus Valley cities were flourishing at the same time Stonehenge was being built in Britain. However, ancient Europe had no cities to match those of Africa and Asia.

HOW DO WE KNOW?

In about 1830, Charles Masson (a deserter from the British Army) was roaming in India when he found brick mounds that looked like old castles. He'd rediscovered ancient Harappa. Later, in 1919, Rakal Das Banerji, an Indian **archaeologist**, found Mohenjo-Daro.

Indus picture-seals were used to stamp impressions in clay, for record-keeping. Hundreds of these seals have been found.

How big was the Indus civilization?

The Indus Valley civilization was bigger than Sumer or ancient Egypt. With an area of 1.3 million square kilometres (500,000 square miles), it covered what is now Afghanistan, Pakistan and northwest India. We're not sure how many people lived in the Indus Valley. Estimates range from 1 to 5 million. The biggest cities were Mohenjo-Daro and Harappa. Mohenjo-Daro was home to 30,000 to 50,000 people, perhaps more.

What was Indus life like?

Today visitors to Mohenjo-Daro swelter in 38 degree Celsius (100 degree Fahrenheit) desert heat. Five thousand years ago, the Indus Valley was probably greener, with more trees and animals such as elephants, rhinoceroses, antelope, water buffalo and tigers. Farmers grew crops using water from the rivers, in order to feed workers living in cities.

Cities were remarkably well-planned, with streets, brick houses and excellent **sanitation**. Skilled workers made goods that were traded into central Asia, Mesopotamia and along the shores of the Arabian Sea. Indus skills and technology involved writing, maths, sculpture, **seals**, bricks, boats, carts, pottery, jewellery and metal tools. Life in the Indus cities seems to have been prosperous and peaceful, from about 2500 to 1700 BC.

Indus cities had a **citadel**, like a castle, on an earth mound. At Mohenjo-Daro and Harappa, the citadels overlooked the "lower town".

Archaeological finds suggest that people lived west of the Indus River by about 8000 BC. They were herders and farmers moving from place to place. Later, people began to settle in villages in the Indus Valley. The river floods (like those of the River Nile in Egypt) provided rich soils for crops. Villages grew into towns in the river **delta**, and later, from around 2600 BC, the Indus people started to build walled cities.

Why city life was good

Living in a city had advantages. A city was a centre for government and trade, where people could develop special skills in making pottery and metal tools. City dwellers felt safe living inside brick and earth walls with watchtowers and gates to protect them from enemies or wild animals. At the city gates, officials could check traders and farmers going in and out of the city – a sign of a settled, organized way of life.

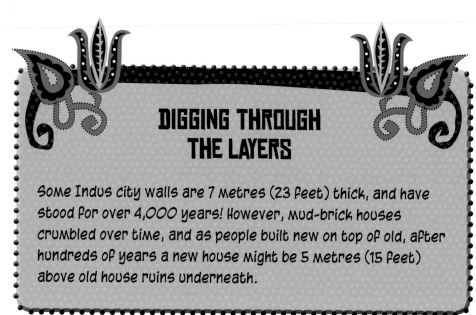

DIGGING THROUGH THE LAYERS

Some Indus city walls are 7 metres (23 feet) thick, and have stood for over 4,000 years! However, mud-brick houses crumbled over time, and as people built new on top of old, after hundreds of years a new house might be 5 metres (15 feet) above old house ruins underneath.

The Indus city of
Mohenjo-Daro today.
The name means
"mound of the dead"
in the Sindhi language,
but these streets once
bustled with life.

City planning

Indus Valley cities shared the same features. Many buildings were raised on earth mounds or platforms of mud-brick, which kept them dry if the river flooded. Straight roads ran north–south and east–west, dividing the city into blocks. The main street was almost 10 metres (33 feet) wide, enough for two carts to pass. Side streets were only 1 metre (3.3 feet) across, with the house walls either side, so the street was shaded from the sun. Narrow alleys led to the front doors of family houses.

Upper town

The upper part of town had the highest mound and the citadel, which was perhaps where the rulers lived. Here there were public buildings, maybe for city government, and the biggest houses. Most homes had a bath area, and brick drains carried water and waste into sewers laid along the streets. There were private and public **wells** for water – Mohenjo-Daro had as many as 3,000 houses, and one in three homes in this city had its own well. Good sanitation was important.

Lower town

Poor people, including most city workers, lived and worked in the larger "lower town" district. Here there were more mounds with buildings on top, and a network of busy streets, markets, workshops and rows of small houses.

Streets like this one in Harappa were once filled with people and carts.

HOW DO WE KNOW?

Excavation of the port-city of Lothal was begun in 1955 by the Archaeological Survey of India. The team, led by S.R. Rao, found a warehouse, factories that made beads, a large brick-lined water tank and also private baths (with paved pathways) - probably for rich citizens.

This artist's picture shows what an Indus city probably looked like.

An "empire of cities"

The Indus Valley was as big as an empire, with more than 1,400 towns and cities besides Mohenjo-Daro and Harappa, including Lothal, Dholavira, Kalibangan and Surkotada. These were not the names used by Indus people. We may never know the original Indus placenames.

Water for trade and life

Lothal is now over 16 kilometres (10 miles) from the sea. But at the time of the Indus civilization, it might have been a busy port. Archaeologists have found a large brick-lined water tank at Lothal that people have suggested was either a dock, reservoir or a **ritual** water tank.

Water was precious, and Indus people were skilled in using and conserving water. Their cities had reservoirs and deep wells. The city of Dholavira was in a very dry region and its people cut more than 15 "water tanks" out of rock to store water brought in channels from rivers. Mohenjo-Daro, the largest Indus city, had 700 wells, and some were 20 metres (66 feet) deep!

HOW DO WE KNOW?

Archaeologists do not always agree on what they find. Some think the 213-metre (700-foot) brick "basin" at Lothal was a dockyard, possibly a repair dock for ships. Others believe it was a reservoir for drinking water.

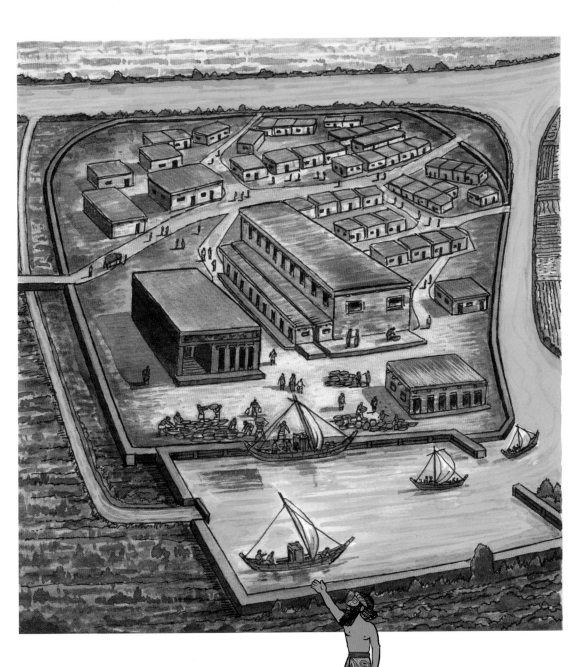

This picture shows what the port of Lothal may have looked like, with ships being loaded and unloaded.

The Great Bath at
Mohenjo-Daro was
probably used for
ritual bathing.

Mohenjo-Daro

Mohenjo-Daro was slightly larger than the northern city of Harappa, and much more of the original city has survived. Each of Mohenjo-Daro's 12 city blocks covers an area of about 300 x 200 metres (91 x 61 feet). Its imposing citadel stood on a mound about 12 metres (40 feet) high, and inside were a large residence (possibly a ruler's home), a food store or granary, and a meeting hall, perhaps for religious ceremonies.

This city has a "Great Bath" that is 12 metres (39 feet) long and 7 metres (23 feet) wide, and once had water 2.4 metres (8 feet) deep. The bath was lined with layers of brick, mortar and bitumen (tar). It had wooden steps for people to enter the water, which came in from a well and flowed out through a drain.

Harappa

Harappa may have been a northern Indus capital. This city also had a citadel-platform with towers and terraces, and a main gate in a wall 9 metres (29 feet) thick. Its large granary or grain-store, workshops and furnaces for metal working show that it was a busy commercial centre.

HOW DO WE KNOW?

Many burials have been found at Indus sites. In the 1920s, archaeologists found 39 skeletons at Mohenjo-Daro. Two skeletons had cut marks, as if made by a sword or spear. Were these the remains of people killed in battle? However, medical evidence showed neither wound was fatal. If these were victims of disease, why were the people not buried in the city graveyard? We may never know the answer to this particular mystery.

WHO RULED THE INDUS PEOPLE?

The Indus Valley was like an empire, but without an emperor – so far as we know. Ancient cities usually had strong kings or priests in charge, yet we have little evidence to show who ruled the Indus people. Indus writing might give clues, but no one has been able to decipher it. Possibly the Indus Valley had a priest-king, like the pharaoh in Egypt. Maybe there were twin capital cities: Mohenjo-Daro and Harappa. Perhaps each city had its own government, like the city-states of ancient Greece.

Organization

A city of 50,000 people needs a city government. All Indus cities were laid out in much the same way, with streets, markets, workshops, public areas and private homes. This required organization.

Trade was also organized. Traders used standard weights to weigh goods. Builders used same-size bricks and measuring rods. Potters crafted pots in the Indus style. So who made the rules? No one knows if Indus people voted for city councils, or just did what their rulers told them.

Did Indus cities have soldiers?

Strong walls usually mean defences, to keep out enemies. Like a medieval castle, an Indus city had towers and gateways, probably with guards to check travellers who tried to pass through. Indus weapons included stone clubs, **copper** or **bronze** swords and knives, and bows and arrows. However, with no history texts or pictures, we don't know for sure if Indus Valley soldiers went to war.

The Indus people made weapons like these from copper and bronze. Some people kept weapons at home, maybe to guard their jewellery and gold!

This stone lamp from Mohenjo-Daro has a woman's head. Perhaps it shows a "mother-goddess".

Were there Indus gods?

The Indus Valley people do not appear to have built huge temples, or if they did, none has survived. Yet there is evidence of religious belief, such as the Great Bath at Mohenjo-Daro, which was possibly used for ritual bathing (see page 15). There are stone carvings, many small **terracotta** figures and images on seals, which all appear to show gods. We have seen that people buried their dead with some of the dead person's most treasured possessions, such as pottery and jewellery. This suggests a belief in life after death.

It is likely that Indus religion had many gods. People made clay images of male and female gods, and also of other human-animal **deities**. They may even have kept small god-statues at home. Many homes contained figures of a female "mother goddess". The pipal or fig tree, seen in many Indus seals, is today a sacred tree for many people in South Asia, suggesting this belief may have been passed down through the generations.

The Priest-King

A small stone statue, found at Mohenjo-Daro in 1927, shows a man wearing a robe with a three-leaf pattern. He has a beard, headband and cloak, and he's come to be known as the "Priest-King". Perhaps the cities of the Indus Valley were ruled by priests, but we don't know for sure.

The Priest-King's statue is only 18 centimetres (7 inches) high. It's one of the few images of an Indus person to have survived.

An Indus Valley house had brick walls. It had a flat roof of wooden beams covered with reeds and clay. Some houses had two stories, with brick stairs between the levels. Many families lived in two-room houses, but larger houses had several rooms around a courtyard, while the very rich had mansions with 30 or more rooms. Mud-bricks crumble, especially after heavy rain or floods, so householders were kept busy with repairs, and brickmakers were never short of work.

This cut-away drawing shows the structure of an Indus city house, which was made from timber and mud bricks.

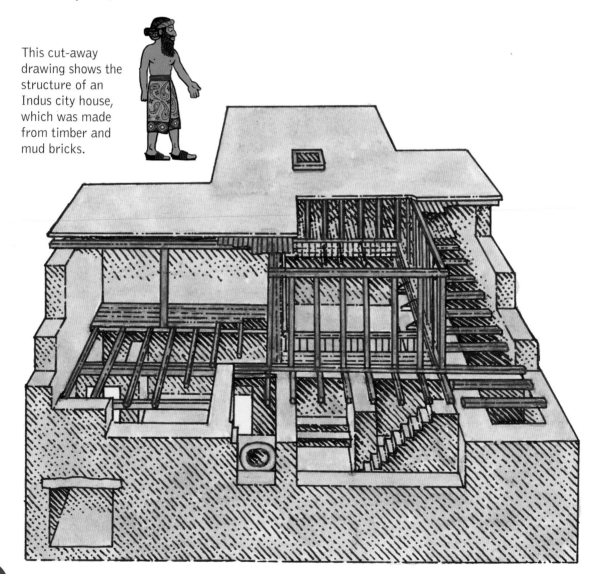

Behind mud walls

High walls gave privacy. The Indus city house had a street door, but no windows opening on to the street. Most houses had small bathrooms, with brick floors, drains and toilets that emptied through clay pipes into street sewers. The street sewers were covered with brick slabs and drained into soak-pits, which someone had to clean – not the nicest job in an Indus city!

House walls were plastered with mud, but it's not clear if there were any wall decorations, such as painting. We can tell from small clay model houses put in graves that windows probably had shutters with grilles to let in cooling air.

Indus brickmakers

Indus brickmakers pressed soft mud into wooden moulds, and turned out the bricks to dry in the hot sun. For harder bricks, they burned or "fired" bricks in a wood-burning **kiln**. All Indus Valley bricks were made to a standard size [about 7 cm x 15 cm x 30 cm/2.75 in. x 5.9 in. x 11.8 in.]. The ratio [height x width x length] was always the same: 1:2:4.

Most workers lived in small terraced houses, with two rooms. Thick brick walls kept houses cool. Niches (hollows) in outside walls could have been used for oil lamps at night, or for statues of gods, placed there to watch over the home.

People still go to the local well to fetch water and meet friends.

Home comforts

Rooms had stone or earth floors, and there was a hearth for cooking, although people could also have cooked food on the roof. Indus furniture hasn't survived, but we can guess that people had simple wooden stools and tables, shelves and chests. Beds were probably made of wood or brick and softened with straw mattresses, animal skins, woollen blankets and (for the rich) cotton textiles. For cooking and storing food, people used pottery jars and dishes, and bowls and pans made from copper or bronze.

Water

In the bathroom, people bathed by pouring water over their bodies from large jars. Many homes had their own wells, but poor people carried water in jars from a communal well. Pieces of broken clay cups found around public wells suggest people gathered for a chat and a drink while fetching water for the family.

Growing food

Indus people ate mostly vegetables and fruit, with some fish and a little meat. Plant remains, such as seeds, show us what crops were grown. Bones are evidence of domestic animals, which included humped cattle (still common in India), sheep and goats. There were chickens, too, domesticated from wild jungle fowl. Water buffalo were either domesticated or hunted in the wild. Hunters brought in forest game, such as antelope, while rivers, canals and the ocean provided fish, shellfish and turtles.

Asian farmers harvest millet, a cereal crop we know was grown by farmers in the Indus civilization.

The rivers' seasonal floods and skilful irrigation meant good farm crops and plenty of food for the cities. The main grain crops were wheat and barley. Wild rice, field peas, lentils, grapes, dates, melons, mustard seeds and sesame were also grown.

Clothes

Indus workers were probably the first in the world to make cotton textiles – for which India is still famous. Indus cotton plants didn't produce much cotton, so cotton cloth would have been an expensive luxury.

From studying Indus figurines (small statues) and scraps of preserved cloth, we can guess that poor people wore few clothes. Women maybe wore a long dress, while men wore a loincloth or kilt. Rich people (the "Priest-King", for instance) wore robes and cloaks, dyed in bright colours. Rich citizens would have worn lots of jewellery and had fancy hairstyles, too.

HOW DO WE KNOW?

Bones found in ancient rubbish dumps tell us what meat Indus people ate. They liked beef, lamb and goat. They hunted antelope and wild pigs, too. Bone remains also show they kept cats and dogs, and had asses and camels - but horses were very rare. Medical tests on skeletons' teeth suggest men ate better than women - Indus women's teeth show evidence of disease linked to **malnutrition**.

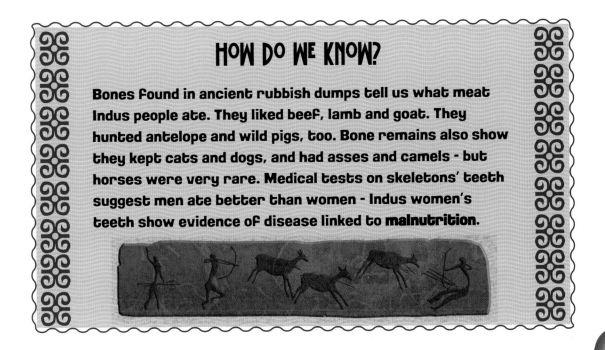

There were many jobs in the Indus Valley. Living in cities mean more people did specialized jobs, and became expert in their skill or craft.

City workers

City workers included builders, craftworkers, officials whose job it was to see that traders stuck to the rules, and rubbish-clearers who kept drains and wells clean. Most of these city workers were probably men.

Family life

Farming and food gathering was an essential task for all the family in the Indus Valley. Children started work young. We don't really know what Indus Valley schools were like. However, we can assume that most children were educated, as **scribes** had to have learned to write, and traders and builders needed to know basic maths. Most children probably followed their parents into the family trade.

The beadmakers

Indus beadmakers made red beads by heating carnelian stones in an oven. The fierce heat turned the brown stone red. After it had cooled, the beadmaker chipped the stone to the desired shape. He or she often painted designs on the beads, using a mixture made from caper tree shoots and salts that turned white when the bead was heated.

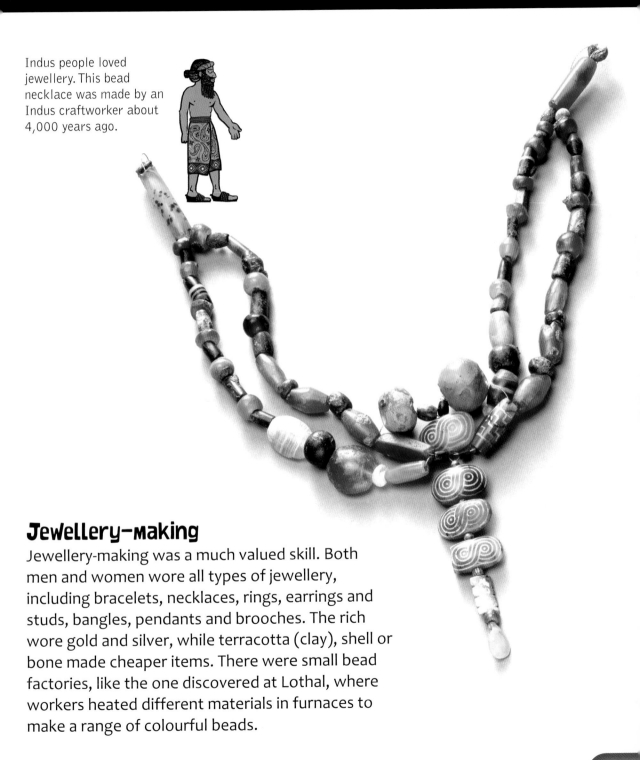

Indus people loved jewellery. This bead necklace was made by an Indus craftworker about 4,000 years ago.

Jewellery-making

Jewellery-making was a much valued skill. Both men and women wore all types of jewellery, including bracelets, necklaces, rings, earrings and studs, bangles, pendants and brooches. The rich wore gold and silver, while terracotta (clay), shell or bone made cheaper items. There were small bead factories, like the one discovered at Lothal, where workers heated different materials in furnaces to make a range of colourful beads.

Clay pots were made on wooden potter's wheels and fired in wood-burning kilns. Cheap pots could be dried in the sun, to save wood.

Pottery

Indus pottery was made in huge amounts, almost as "mass-production" lines. Most pots were for everyday use, ranging from large storage jars to small dishes and bowls in plain terracotta, but some were decorated in black on red, or cream on black and red. Special pots were painted with leaves, flowers, birds and fish scale patterns. One common pot shape is a flat dish on an "offering stand", perhaps for religious use.

Seals

The Indus Valley people are famous for their seals. Hundreds of these small pieces have been found. They look like tags, no more than 2.5 centimetres (1 inch) long. Many were made of steatite (a soft stone) or faience (a ceramic), though a few were made from copper or silver metal. Seals have carved images of animals, plants or human figures. For example, one seal shows a woman fighting animals and another shows a horned hunter attacking a tiger.

Other trades

Carpenters made wooden furniture and handles for tools, such as hoes and axes. Metalworkers made tools from copper and bronze: arrowheads, knives, razors, saws, fish-hooks, chisels and needles. They made mirrors, too, and cast statues in molten metal using the lost-wax process (see page 39 for more on this).

This seal shows a man with two tigers. Seals may have been worn as good luck charms or used as "labels" for traded goods.

POO POTS

An Indus potter might be seen collecting goat poo. This wasn't to use as manure in his garden, but to mix with his clay. Goat dung was used to give pots a dark tint!

A clay model of a bullock cart. Carts like these are still used in India and Pakistan.

Trade and transport

Trade was essential to Indus Valley cities. Traders brought in the **raw materials** that city workers needed. City workers used these materials to make pots, beads, tools, jewellery and cotton cloth.

Sourcing raw materials often meant a very long journey. **Minerals** came from Iran and Afghanistan. Lead and copper came from India. Cedar tree wood was floated down the rivers from Kashmir and the Himalayan Mountains. **Jade** came over the mountains from China.

Trade by barter

The Indus people didn't use money, instead they traded by "barter" – the buyer and seller made a deal, and exchanged goods. They weighed items on balance scales, using stone cubes as weights.

Travel

Archaeologists have found clay models of Indus carts. These wooden carts would have been loaded with grain, vegetables and fruit, and pulled by bullocks. Roads were muddy when it rained, dusty when dry, and usually tough going. For heavy loads, boats were the fastest means of transportation. Going downriver was easiest, following the flow of the river to the ocean.

CHECKING BY WEIGHT

For weighing on scales, traders used as weights cubes of a rock called grey chert. The smallest cube weighed less than 1 gram (0.03 ounces). The weights system was complex, apparently based both on "doubling" (1,2,4,8...) and decimal (0.05, 0.1, 0.2, 0.5, 1, 2...). The Indus measuring system included a measure of about 33 centimetres (13.2 inches), similar to 12 inches (the imperial foot).

A useful measuring tool was a metal rod marked off in divisions of 7 millimetres (0.3 inches). The Indus people were obviously good at maths!

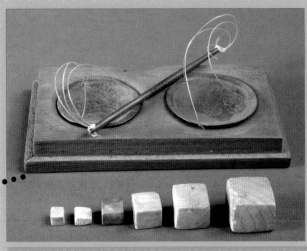

Here are a set of balance scales with Indus stone weights.

Even without money, trade was very important in the Indus Valley civilization. Traders were keen to sell goods made in the cities. They were often away from home for weeks or months, heading off to find raw materials, to make deals and to find new markets for the many items that Indus people made with such skill. Important trade items included pottery, semi-precious stones such as turquoise and lapis lazuli, silver and gold, lead and tin, flints (for making stone tools), ivory combs and pearls.

Traders crossed mountains and forests. They followed rivers, walking along the river bank. They often travelled in a group, or "caravan", with a string of camels or asses to carry the heavy loads. It was safer to travel in this way when passing through jungle where tigers roamed, or in mountains where bandits lurked. Travellers set off early in the morning before it got too hot, rested during the midday heat, then camped at night. Sometimes they used one of the hotels along trade routes.

Lapis lazuli, a beautiful blue gemstone, was traded from the mountains in Afghanistan.

Indus traders used pack
animals, such as camels,
for long overland journeys.

New contacts

Traders made long journeys
from the Indus Valley to
foreign lands, travelling
by sea. These trade links
extended as far west as
Mesopotamia (modern Iraq).
Through these contacts,
other civilizations learned of
the wealth and skills of Indus
culture.

A FISH DISH

Archaeologists found hundreds of
fish skulls in one Indus rubbish dump.
Perhaps it was a factory, where fish
were dried or salted to preserve them.
Dried fish would have been a useful
packed lunch for a travelling trader!

This seal shows a one-horned bull, which people once thought might be a unicorn! You can see some Indus writing above the bull.

Twin cities

Mesopotamia, "the land between two rivers" (the Tigris and Euphrates), was rich and powerful, and ready to trade. Traders from Mesopotamia came to live in Indus cities, and Indus merchants went to live in Mesopotamia.

The puzzle of Indus writing

Indus traders carried valuable cargo, such as cotton and beads, to exchange for bitumen tar in Mesopotamia (which had a lot of oil). They took seals, and perhaps clay tablets with written messages from their rulers. Unfortunately, although many seals have been found, no one has been able to make sense of the writing. Indus people wrote by making marks and pictures, and each picture-symbol probably represents a word or part of a word.

The first line of text was written from right to left, the second line from left to right, and so on. There were at least 400 characters (letters, signs and numbers), but the longest text found has only 26. There are no long books. Indus writing is an unreadable puzzle for now – but if we ever unravel the code or find more writing, we'll discover a lot more about these amazing people.

Boats like this carried traders on rivers and oceans. They sailed along the shores of the Arabian Sea, keeping sight of land, if they could, until they reached port.

The people from Meluhha

A king of the Akkad empire who ruled in Sumer, Mesopotamia (now Iraq), had his scribes keep note of who came to his kingdom. We can read Sumerian writing, so we have learned that traders came to Akkad from Meluhha (the Indus Valley). Bits of Indus pottery found on beaches in the Persian Gulf tell us that Indus traders left them, probably stopping off when sailing west to Mesopotamia.

Many children worked as soon as they were big enough to help on farms and in workshops. However, there was time for games and toys. Small figures, models and toys made from baked clay and metal have been found, though they could also bear some religious significance. There are wheeled carts, some with a roof to keep people cool, or dry when it rained. Model cows waggle their heads when a string is pulled, toy monkeys slide down ropes, and there are toy squirrels and other animals.

These clay models of a lion and horse from Mohenjo-Daro are now in a museum in India.

An ancient Indus board game, from the Harappa Museum in Pakistan.

Games and sports

Indus people played board games with dice and counters. They had pets, including cats and dogs, which left paw-prints in wet mud-bricks (the paw-print was preserved when the mud hardened). Archaeologists have even discovered a preserved monkey paw-print!

Living close to water, people must have enjoyed boating, fishing and even swimming, though they had to watch out for crocodiles and snakes! They could explore the forest, or go hunting in the marshes with bows and arrows, and slingshots (stone-throwers). Roast duck and fish netted in the river made a tasty barbecue!

DOUBLE SIX WINS

At Harappa, archaeologists found dice made from cubes of sandstone and terracotta. These could well be the oldest dice in the world, and are practically the same as dice today, with six sides and spots for 1 to 6.

Art and social life

There is not a lot of Indus art left, apart from pictures on seals, decorated pottery and small clay figures. Any big carved statues or wall-art, as seen in later Indian architecture, have long ago been destroyed. All that survive are small pieces of art, like the bronze figure of a girl who looks as if she's dancing.

Party time?

Dancing girls may have entertained at feasts or city festivals. From the scraps of evidence from pottery and sculpture, we see that rich women wore patterned cotton robes, expensive jewellery and had elegant hairstyles. We can imagine them visiting friends' houses to celebrate a wedding or a new baby. Dancing to the music of pipes, drums and stringed instruments is also a big part of the traditional culture of South and Central Asia.

A good life

Indus people worked hard, and most had little spare time. Yet the Indus Valley seems to have enjoyed a settled period of hundreds of years, so its people were left at peace to enjoy their streets, markets and private bathrooms. Probably most could relax in the evening after work, and feel that life was on the whole pretty good.

This figure of an Indus woman was found at Mohenjo-Daro. Was she a temple priestess or perhaps a **slave**?

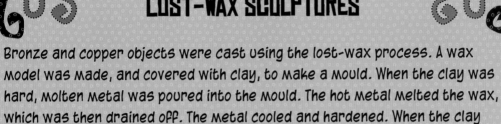

LOST-WAX SCULPTURES

Bronze and copper objects were cast using the lost-wax process. A wax model was made, and covered with clay, to make a mould. When the clay was hard, molten metal was poured into the mould. The hot metal melted the wax, which was then drained off. The metal cooled and hardened. When the clay mould was broken off, a metal casting of the original model was revealed.

Terracotta models like this were made as children's toys.

The Indus civilization changed little in 800 years. Then, between 1800 and 1500 BC, it went into decline. By 1300 BC it had ended. Why? No one is sure. There is no evidence of war. So what happened?

Old and new are often seen side by side in modern India and Pakistan.

40

The pipal or fig tree was a sacred tree in the Indus Valley and is still held sacred by people across South Asia today.

Possible reasons

The decline of the Indus Valley may have been due to several reasons. Maybe the population just got too big, food got scarce and people began to starve. Some experts suggest that if some rivers altered course, or dried up, cities were left without water, and people without enough food. Maybe terrible floods, or even an earthquake, brought disaster. Perhaps an epidemic of disease killed thousands of people and the survivors had to move on. Another possibility is that enemies attacked the cities.

The end

By 1500 BC, the Indus Valley civilization was crumbling. Most people lived in villages, and traders no longer sailed to Mesopotamia and other lands. In time, even the brick walls and buildings were no more, as new civilizations came and went during the long history of India and Pakistan. Yet much of Indus tradition lived on in the culture, art and religion of the sub-continent. Modern cities bustle with traffic and hi-tech commerce, and trade remains at the heart of South Asian life. However, in a world of cars and computers, you can still see bullock carts and camels plodding dusty roads, just as they did 5,000 years ago.

A day in the life of an Indus boy

Hi, my name is Arshad and I live in Mohenjo-Daro. My dad's one of the city's best brickmakers, and he's gone up to the Great Bath to do some repairs. My mum and my two sisters are washing clothes on the riverbank. Usually I help Dad, but he said there might be priests at the Bath, to check the work, and I might get into mischief.

For breakfast, I had a slice of juicy melon, and a chunk of Mum's bread, freshly baked. My friends and I are going to the market, and we'll stop at the well for a drink. We like to see the traders – and the hunters, too. Last week we saw a man with a tiger cub, and a dancing monkey! Mum has given me one of the little seed necklaces she makes, so I can trade for some lunch – maybe some salt fish, or a dish of turtle stew.

We've come down to the river – but not where the women are washing. We like to see the boats, and the men unloading all the sacks while officials check the seals. My uncle is a sealmaker – it's really clever, the way he carves those pictures and the wiggly writing. I'm hoping he will teach me.

Yesterday I saw a crocodile! So we'd better watch out near the water. Our country cousins have come to the city to trade wool and sheep meat. They're going to eat supper with us, and we'll swap news. It's a long walk home to their village. I'm glad our house is in town – it's so hot tonight, I think I'll sleep on the flat roof and see how many stars I can count...

AROUND 9000 BC

The first farmers plant crops and raise domestic animals. Living in one place, rather than as wandering nomads, means people build permanent settlements. The first cities are built, including Jericho and Catal Huyuk (in the Near East).

4500 BC

Civilizations are beginning in Sumer (Mesopotamia) and Egypt, with people building cities close to rivers

4000 BC

People settle in the Indus Valley, and begin to make copper tools and clay pots

3300 BC

Mohenjo-Daro is a village, but is beginning to grow into a city

3200 BC

The earliest writing dates from about this time, made by drawing pictures and marks on clay

3000 BC

People in several civilizations, including the Indus Valley, have invented the wheel and are using wheeled carts pulled by animals

2750 BC

In Great Britain, people start building at Stonehenge

2600 BC

At about this time the Egyptians are building the first pyramids

2500 BC

Indus Valley people are building large cities such as Harappa, Mohenjo-Daro, Chanhu-Daro and Dholavira. The cities have brick walls, baths, food stores, water supplies, drains, and flourishing arts and crafts.

2350 BC

Sargon of Akkad, a great king in Sumer (Mesopotamia), rules an empire which trades with the Indus Valley. Indus traders travel by land and sea to make contacts with Mesopotamia and other cultures.

2000 BC

Indus cities are rich and busy, and the Indus civilization covers a vast area. People make all kinds of goods, including beads, pots and metal tools. Traders use seals, with writing. Priest-kings possibly rule the cities.

1900–1700 BC

Hard times begin for the Indus Valley cities. Repair work and new building stops. Possible reasons for this decline include rivers drying up, or floods. Famine may have forced people to move away.

1500 BC

Some people think northern invaders called Aryans moved into the Indus Valley about this time, to hasten the end of the Indus civilization

1300 BC

Mohenjo-Daro and other Indus cities crumble into ruins. The Indus Valley civilization ends, but much of the culture is passed on.

AROUND 1830

British explorer Charles Masson finds the ruins of Harappa. In the 1850s, many of its ancient bricks are removed to build a railway.

1919

Mohenjo-Daro is rediscovered by Indian archaeologist Rakal Das Banerji. Archaeologists in the 1930s, and from the 1950s to the present, uncover more fascinating facts, and mysteries, about this lost civilization.

GLOSSARY

archaeologist person who studies the bones, tools and other objects of ancient people to learn about past human life and activities

bronze metal made by mixing copper and tin

citadel fortlike building, usually in a raised position in an Indus city

civilization culture and society of a region at a particular time

copper metal used by ancient peoples to make tools, and still used today

deity (plural: deities) god or goddess

delta mouth of a river and the land around it

evidence materials or facts that can help us make a conclusion about something

excavation dig underground at a site in order to uncover the past

irrigation system of canals that carries water from a river or lake to crops in fields

jade hard stone used to make jewellery and ornaments

kiln very hot oven used to bake and harden materials such as clay pots and bricks

malnutrition lacking nutrients, the result of not having enough to eat or not eating the right things

mineral natural substance such as gold, silver, stone or sand

raw material material or resource, such as timber or minerals, which people use for building or making things

ritual religious ceremony or action performed in the same way each time

sanitation process by which water is kept clean and waste is disposed of safely, preventing harm to humans

scribe person who could read and write, who often served as a high official

seal small stone tag with a picture that left an impression when stamped into soft clay

slave person who is not free and has to work for an owner for no payment

terracotta form of pottery made from clay baked at a high temperature in order to make it hard and waterproof

well deep hole dug to find and extract water from underground

Books

Indus Valley City (Building History), Gillian Clements (Franklin Watts, 2004)
The Indus Valley (Excavating the Past), Ilona Aronovsky and Sujata Gopinath
(Heinemann, 2004)
The Indus Valley (The History Detective Investigates), Claudia Martin (Wayland, 2014)

Websites

www.ancientindia.co.uk
This British Museum site looks at the prehistory of India and the Indus Valley
civilization. You can spend a day with an Indus beadmaker's son and explore the city
of Mohenjo-Daro.
www.bbc.co.uk/schools/primaryhistory/indus_valley
This BBC site looks at aspects of Indus life, with games and a quiz.
http://mocomi.com/indus-valley-civilization
This site takes an animated look at the Indus Valley culture.

Places to visit

Ashmolean Museum of Art and Archaeology
Beaumont St
Oxford
OX1 2PH
www.ashmolean.org

Here you can see Indus Valley terracotta items, such as beakers from the cities of
Mohenjo-Daro and Chanhudaro.

British Museum
Great Russell Street
London
WC1B 3DG
www.britishmuseum.org

The place to look is the South Asia Gallery, where you can also find later Indian
civilizations represented.

INDEX